MW01680447

brauerskb@yahoo.com.
Kt2TRoyWI2

Just The facts101

Textbook Key Facts

Textbook Outlines, Highlights, and Practice Quizzes

Adult Development and Aging

by John C. Cavanaugh, 7th Edition

All "Just the Facts101" Material Written or Prepared by Cram101 Textbook Reviews

Title Page

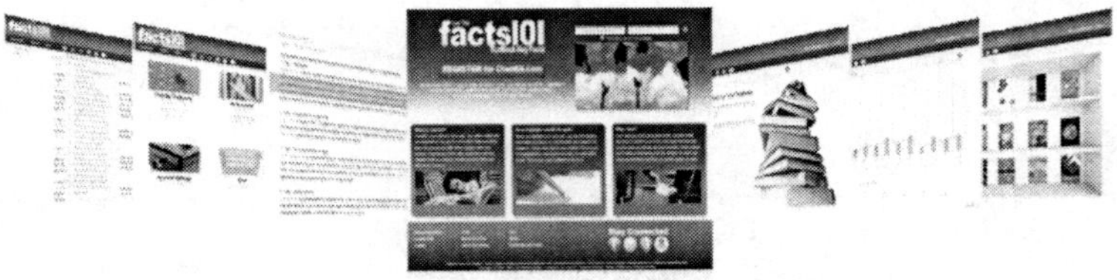
facts101

facts101
LEARNING SYSTEM

"Just the Facts101" is a Content Technologies publication and tool designed to give you all the facts from your textbooks. Visit JustTheFacts101.com for the full practice test for each of your chapters for virtually any of your textbooks.

Facts101 has built custom study tools specific to your textbook. We provide all of the factual testable information and unlike traditional study guides, we will never send you back to your textbook for more information.

YOU WILL NEVER HAVE TO HIGHLIGHT A BOOK AGAIN!

Facts101 StudyGuides
All of the information in this StudyGuide is written specifically for your textbook. We include the key terms, places, people, and concepts... the information you can expect on your next exam!

Want to take a practice test?
Throughout each chapter of this StudyGuide you will find links to JustTheFacts101.com where you can select specific chapters to take a complete test on, or you can subscribe and get practice tests for up to 12 of your textbooks, along with other exclusive Jtf101.com tools like problem solving labs and reference libraries.

JustTheFacts101.com
Only Jtf101.com gives you the outlines, highlights, and PRACTICE TESTS specific to your textbook. JustTheFacts101.com is an online application where you'll discover study tools designed to make the most of your limited study time.

By purchasing this book, you get 50% off the normal monthly subscription fee!. Just enter the promotional code **'DK73DW24648'** on the Jtf101.com registration screen.

www.JustTheFacts101.com

ISBN(s): 9781497001763. PUBE-6.2014423

Adult Development and Aging
John C. Cavanaugh, 7th

CONTENTS

1. Studying Adult Development and Aging

CHAPTER OUTLINE: KEY TERMS, PEOPLE, PLACES, CONCEPTS

________	Ageism
________	Adolescence
________	Human development
________	Personality
________	Generation X
________	Lesbian
________	Dependency ratio
________	Longevity
________	Erectile dysfunction

CHAPTER HIGHLIGHTS & NOTES: KEY TERMS, PEOPLE, PLACES, CONCEPTS

Ageism	Ageism is stereotyping and discriminating against individuals or groups on the basis of their age. This may be casual or systematic. The term was coined in 1969 by Robert Neil Butler to describe discrimination against seniors, and patterned on sexism and racism.
Adolescence	Adolescence is a transitional stage of physical and psychological human development that generally occurs during the period from puberty to legal adulthood (age of majority). The period of adolescence is most closely associated with the teenage years, though its physical, psychological and cultural expressions may begin earlier and end later. For example, although puberty has been historically associated with the onset of adolescent development, it now typically begins prior to the teenage years and there has been a normative shift of it occurring in preadolescence, particularly in females .
Human development	Human development is the process of growing to maturity. In biological terms, this entails growth from a one-celled zygote to an adult human being.
Personality	Personality is the particular combination of emotional, attitudinal, and behavioral response patterns of an individual.

Different personality theorists present their own definitions of the word based on their theoretical positions. Psychologists such as Freud, and Erik Erikson have attempted to come up with personality theories.

Generation X

Generation X, commonly abbreviated to Gen X, is the generation born after the Western Post-World War II baby boom. Demographers, historians and commentators use beginning birth dates from the early 1960s to the early 1980s.

Lesbian

Lesbian is the term most widely used in the English language to describe romantic or sexual attraction between women. The word may be used as a noun, to refer to women who identify themselves or who are characterized by others as having the primary attribute of female homosexuality, or as an adjective, to describe characteristics of an object or activity related to female same-sex attraction.

'Lesbian' as a concept, used to differentiate women with a shared sexual orientation, is a 20th-century construct.

Dependency ratio

In economics, geography and demography the dependency ratio is an age-population ratio of those typically not in the labor force and those typically in the labor force (the productive part). It is used to measure the pressure on productive population.

Longevity

The word 'longevity' is sometimes used as a synonym for 'life expectancy' in demography - however, the term 'longevity' is sometimes meant to refer only to especially long lived members of a population, whereas 'life expectancy' is always defined statistically as the average number of years remaining at a given age. For example, a population's life expectancy at birth is the same as the average age at death for all people born in the same year (in the case of cohorts). Longevity is best thought of as a term for general audiences meaning 'typical length of life' and specific statistical definitions should be clarified when necessary.

Erectile dysfunction

Erectile dysfunction or impotence is sexual dysfunction characterized by the inability to develop or maintain an erection of the penis during sexual performance.

A penile erection is the hydraulic effect of blood entering and being retained in sponge-like bodies within the penis. The process is often initiated as a result of sexual arousal, when signals are transmitted from the brain to nerves in the penis.

1. _________ is the process of growing to maturity. In biological terms, this entails growth from a one-celled zygote to an adult human being.

   a. Bairn
   b. Barrel children
   c. Behavior Rating Inventory of Executive Function
   d. Human development

2. _________ is a transitional stage of physical and psychological human development that generally occurs during the period from puberty to legal adulthood (age of majority). The period of _________ is most closely associated with the teenage years, though its physical, psychological and cultural expressions may begin earlier and end later. For example, although puberty has been historically associated with the onset of adolescent development, it now typically begins prior to the teenage years and there has been a normative shift of it occurring in pre_________, particularly in females .

   a. Adolescence
   b. Deinstitutionalisation
   c. Foster care
   d. Foundling hospital

3. In economics, geography and demography the _________ is an age-population ratio of those typically not in the labor force and those typically in the labor force (the productive part). It is used to measure the pressure on productive population.

   a. Beadsman
   b. Cash balance plan
   c. Dependency ratio
   d. Retirement

4. _________ is stereotyping and discriminating against individuals or groups on the basis of their age. This may be casual or systematic. The term was coined in 1969 by Robert Neil Butler to describe discrimination against seniors, and patterned on sexism and racism.

   a. Ageism
   b. Definitions of abortion
   c. Feticide
   d. Late termination of pregnancy

5. . _________ is the particular combination of emotional, attitudinal, and behavioral response patterns of an individual. Different _________ theorists present their own definitions of the word based on their theoretical positions. Psychologists such as Freud, and Erik Erikson have attempted to come up with _________ theories.

   a. Personality
   b. Barry Bogin
   c. Birth order

ANSWER KEY
1. Studying Adult Development and Aging

1. d
2. a
3. c
4. a
5. a

---

2. Neuroscience as a Basis for Adult Development and Aging

CHAPTER OUTLINE: KEY TERMS, PEOPLE, PLACES, CONCEPTS

_______ Cancer

_______ Radical

_______ Sandwich generation

CHAPTER HIGHLIGHTS & NOTES: KEY TERMS, PEOPLE, PLACES, CONCEPTS

Cancer

Cancer , known medically as a malignant neoplasm, is a broad group of diseases involving unregulated cell growth. In cancer, cells divide and grow uncontrollably, forming malignant tumors, and invading nearby parts of the body. The cancer may also spread to more distant parts of the body through the lymphatic system or bloodstream.

Radical

In chemistry, a radical is an atom, molecule, or ion that has unpaired valence electrons or an open electron shell, and therefore may be seen as having one or more 'dangling' covalent bonds.

With some exceptions, these 'dangling' bonds make free radicals highly chemically reactive towards other substances, or even towards themselves: their molecules will often spontaneously dimerize or polymerize if they come in contact with each other. Most radicals are reasonably stable only at very low concentrations in inert media or in vacuum.

Sandwich generation

The Sandwich generation is a generation of people who care for their aging parents while supporting their own children.

According to the Pew Research Center, just over 1 of every 8 Americans aged 40 to 60 is both raising a child and caring for a parent, in addition to between 7 to 10 million adults caring for their aging parents from a long distance. US Census Bureau statistics indicate that the number of older Americans aged 65 or older will double by the year 2030, to over 70 million.

2. Neuroscience as a Basis for Adult Development and Aging

CHAPTER QUIZ: KEY TERMS, PEOPLE, PLACES, CONCEPTS

1. _________ , known medically as a malignant neoplasm, is a broad group of diseases involving unregulated cell growth. In _________, cells divide and grow uncontrollably, forming malignant tumors, and invading nearby parts of the body. The _________ may also spread to more distant parts of the body through the lymphatic system or bloodstream.

   a. Cancer
   b. Definitions of abortion
   c. Feticide
   d. Late termination of pregnancy

2. In chemistry, a _________ is an atom, molecule, or ion that has unpaired valence electrons or an open electron shell, and therefore may be seen as having one or more 'dangling' covalent bonds.

   With some exceptions, these 'dangling' bonds make free _________s highly chemically reactive towards other substances, or even towards themselves: their molecules will often spontaneously dimerize or polymerize if they come in contact with each other. Most _________s are reasonably stable only at very low concentrations in inert media or in vacuum.

   a. Radical
   b. Biomarkers of aging
   c. Brooke Greenberg
   d. Cellular senescence

3. The _________ is a generation of people who care for their aging parents while supporting their own children.

   According to the Pew Research Center, just over 1 of every 8 Americans aged 40 to 60 is both raising a child and caring for a parent, in addition to between 7 to 10 million adults caring for their aging parents from a long distance. US Census Bureau statistics indicate that the number of older Americans aged 65 or older will double by the year 2030, to over 70 million.

   a. Sandwich generation
   b. 386 Generation
   c. Baby boomer
   d. Burnt Generation

ANSWER KEY

2. Neuroscience as a Basis for Adult Development and Aging

---

1. a
2. a
3. a

---

3. Physical Changes

CHAPTER OUTLINE: KEY TERMS, PEOPLE, PLACES, CONCEPTS

- Erectile dysfunction
- Cancer
- Radical
- Sandwich generation
- DNA replication
- Leonard Hayflick
- Telomerase
- Telomere
- Collagen
- Dependency ratio
- Osteoporosis
- Lesbian
- Epilepsy
- Arthritis
- Osteoarthritis
- Rheumatoid arthritis
- Casual sex
- Vertigo
- Heart failure
- Aphasia
- Hemiplegia

3. Physical Changes

CHAPTER OUTLINE: KEY TERMS, PEOPLE, PLACES, CONCEPTS

______ Hypertension

______ Reproductive system

______ Lung

______ Climacteric

______ Menopause

______ Estrogen

______ Menstruation

______ Ovary

______ Ovulation

______ Fall prevention

CHAPTER HIGHLIGHTS & NOTES: KEY TERMS, PEOPLE, PLACES, CONCEPTS

Erectile dysfunction

Erectile dysfunction or impotence is sexual dysfunction characterized by the inability to develop or maintain an erection of the penis during sexual performance.

A penile erection is the hydraulic effect of blood entering and being retained in sponge-like bodies within the penis. The process is often initiated as a result of sexual arousal, when signals are transmitted from the brain to nerves in the penis.

Cancer

Cancer , known medically as a malignant neoplasm, is a broad group of diseases involving unregulated cell growth. In cancer, cells divide and grow uncontrollably, forming malignant tumors, and invading nearby parts of the body. The cancer may also spread to more distant parts of the body through the lymphatic system or bloodstream.

Radical

In chemistry, a radical is an atom, molecule, or ion that has unpaired valence electrons or an open electron shell, and therefore may be seen as having one or more 'dangling' covalent bonds.

With some exceptions, these 'dangling' bonds make free radicals highly chemically reactive towards other substances, or even towards themselves: their molecules will often spontaneously dimerize or polymerize if they come in contact with each other. Most radicals are reasonably stable only at very low concentrations in inert media or in vacuum.

Sandwich generation

The Sandwich generation is a generation of people who care for their aging parents while supporting their own children.

According to the Pew Research Center, just over 1 of every 8 Americans aged 40 to 60 is both raising a child and caring for a parent, in addition to between 7 to 10 million adults caring for their aging parents from a long distance. US Census Bureau statistics indicate that the number of older Americans aged 65 or older will double by the year 2030, to over 70 million.

DNA replication

DNA replication is the process of producing two identical copies from one original DNA molecule. This biological process occurs in all living organisms and is the basis for biological inheritance. DNA is composed of two strands and each strand of the original DNA molecule serves as template for the production of the complementary strand, a process referred to as semiconservative replication.

Leonard Hayflick

Leonard Hayflick, Ph.D., is Professor of Anatomy at the University of California, San Francisco, School of Medicine, and was Professor of Medical Microbiology at Stanford University School of Medicine. He is a past president of the Gerontological Society of America and was a founding member of the council of the National Institute on Aging (NIA). The recipient of several research prizes and awards, including the 1991 Sandoz Prize for Gerontological Research, he has studied the aging process for more than thirty years.

Telomerase

Telomerase is a ribonucleoprotein that is an enzyme that adds DNA sequence repeats to the 3' end of DNA strands in the telomere regions, which are found at the ends of eukaryotic chromosomes. This region of repeated nucleotide called telomeres contains noncoding DNA and hinders the loss of important DNA from chromosome ends. As a result, every time the chromosome is copied, only 100-200 nucleotides are lost, which causes no damage to the organism's DNA. Telomerase is a reverse transcriptase that carries its own RNA molecule, which is used as a template when it elongates telomeres, which are shortened after each replication cycle.

Telomere

A telomere is a region of repetitive nucleotide sequences at each end of a chromatid, which protects the end of the chromosome from deterioration or from fusion with neighboring chromosomes. Its name is derived from the Greek nouns telos (t????) 'end' and mer?s (µ????, root: µe?-) 'part.' Telomere regions deter the degradation of genes near the ends of chromosomes by allowing chromosome ends to shorten, which necessarily occurs during chromosome replication.

3. Physical Changes

CHAPTER HIGHLIGHTS & NOTES: KEY TERMS, PEOPLE, PLACES, CONCEPTS

Collagen	Collagen is the main structural protein of the various connective tissues in animals. (The name collagen comes from the Greek kolla meaning glue and suffix -gen denoting producing). As the main component of connective tissue, it is the most abundant protein in mammals, making up from 25% to 35% of the whole-body protein content.
Dependency ratio	In economics, geography and demography the dependency ratio is an age-population ratio of those typically not in the labor force and those typically in the labor force (the productive part). It is used to measure the pressure on productive population.
Osteoporosis	Osteoporosis is a progressive bone disease that is characterized by a decrease in bone mass and density which can lead to an increased risk of fracture. In osteoporosis, the bone mineral density (BMD) is reduced, bone microarchitecture deteriorates, and the amount and variety of proteins in bone are altered. Osteoporosis is defined by the World Health Organization (WHO) as a bone mineral density of 2.5 standard deviations or more below the mean peak bone mass (average of young, healthy adults) as measured by dual-energy X-ray absorptiometry; the term 'established osteoporosis' includes the presence of a fragility fracture.
Lesbian	Lesbian is the term most widely used in the English language to describe romantic or sexual attraction between women. The word may be used as a noun, to refer to women who identify themselves or who are characterized by others as having the primary attribute of female homosexuality, or as an adjective, to describe characteristics of an object or activity related to female same-sex attraction. 'Lesbian' as a concept, used to differentiate women with a shared sexual orientation, is a 20th-century construct.
Epilepsy	Epilepsy is a common and diverse set of chronic neurological disorders characterized by seizures. It is a paroxysmal behavioral spell generally caused by an excessive disorderly discharge of cortical nerve cells of the brain and can range from clinically undetectable (electrographic seizures) to convulsions. Some definitions of epilepsy require that seizures be recurrent and unprovoked, but others require only a single seizure combined with brain alterations which increase the chance of future seizures.
Arthritis	Arthritis is a form of joint disorder that involves inflammation of one or more joints. There are over 100 different forms of arthritis. The most common form, osteoarthritis is a result of trauma to the joint, infection of the joint, or age.
Osteoarthritis	Osteoarthritis also known as degenerative arthritis or degenerative joint disease or osteoarthrosis, is a group of mechanical abnormalities involving degradation of joints, including articular cartilage and subchondral bone. Symptoms may include joint pain, tenderness, stiffness, locking, and sometimes an effusion.

Rheumatoid arthritis	Rheumatoid arthritis is an autoimmune disease that results in a chronic, systemic inflammatory disorder that may affect many tissues and organs, but principally attacks flexible . It is widely used as an indicator of RA disease activity and response to treatment, but is not always a reliable indicator of treatment effect. The joints included in DAS28 are (bilaterally): proximal interphalangeal joints (10 joints), metacarpophalangeal joints (10), wrists (2), elbows (2), shoulders (2) and knees (2).
Casual sex	Casual sex or hooking up are certain types of human sexual activity outside the context of a romantic relationship. The term is not always used consistently: it may refer to extramarital sex, sex in a casual relationship, one-time encounters, promiscuous sex, or sex in the absence of emotional attachment or love, which can include prostitution and swinging. Other terms sometimes associated with casual sex include recreational sex, social sex, nonrelationship sex, no-strings-attached (NSA) sex, physical relationship, or sex with no games.
Vertigo	Vertigo is the student magazine of the University of Technology, Sydney. Its name derives from the university's main building, which is a 28-storey brutal modernist tower block and how the Vertigo Offices were originally at its summit (they have since been moved to Level 3). The magazine is published by the UTS Students' Association.
Heart failure	Heart failure, often called congestive heart failure or congestive cardiac failure (CCF), occurs when the heart is unable to provide sufficient pump action to maintain blood flow to meet the needs of the body. Heart failure can cause a number of symptoms including shortness of breath, leg swelling, and exercise intolerance. The condition is diagnosed by patient physical examination and confirmed with echocardiography.
Aphasia	Aphasia is a disturbance of the comprehension and formulation of language caused by dysfunction in specific brain regions. This class of language disorder ranges from having difficulty remembering words to losing the ability to speak, read, or write. This also affects visual language such as sign language.
Hemiplegia	Hemiplegia /he.m?.pli?.d?i?/ is paralysis of the arm, leg, and trunk on the same side of the body. Hemiplegia is more severe than hemiparesis, wherein one half of the body has less marked weakness. Hemiplegia and Hemiparesis may be congenital, or they might be acquired conditions resulting from an illness, an injury, or a stroke.
Hypertension	Hypertension or high blood pressure, sometimes called arterial hypertension, is a chronic medical condition in which the blood pressure in the arteries is elevated. This requires the heart to work harder than normal to circulate blood through the blood vessels.

3. Physical Changes

CHAPTER HIGHLIGHTS & NOTES: KEY TERMS, PEOPLE, PLACES, CONCEPTS

Reproductive system	The reproductive system or genital system is a system of sex organs within an organism which work together for the purpose of reproduction. Many non-living substances such as fluids, hormones, and pheromones are also important accessories to the reproductive system. Unlike most organ systems, the sexes of differentiated species often have significant differences.
Lung	Lung means wind or breath. It is a key concept in the Vajrayana traditions of Tibetan Buddhism and has a variety of meanings. Lung is a concept that's particularly important to understandings of the subtle body and the Three Vajras (body, speech and mind).
Climacteric	In current practice, climacteric is most often a synonym for female menopause. In Princeton University's online Wordnet database, climacteric is listed as: •(n) climacteric•(n) menopause, climacteric, change of life (the time in a woman's life in which the menstrual cycle ends) The term is used for both genders by The International Menopause Society, which defines itself as 'The society for the study of all aspects of the climacteric in men and women.'
Menopause	Menopause refers to the time of cessation of a woman's reproductive ability. Menopause literally means the 'end of monthly cycles', from the Greek word pausis (cessation) and the root men- (month). Menopause is an event that typically occurs in women in midlife, during their late 40s or early 50s, and it signals the end of the fertile phase of a woman's life.
Estrogen	Oestrogens or estrogens, are a group of compounds named for their importance in both menstrual and estrous reproductive cycles. They are the primary female sex hormones. Natural estrogens are steroid hormones, while some synthetic ones are non-steroidal.
Menstruation	Menstruation is the periodic discharge of blood and mucosal tissue from the uterus and vagina. It starts at menarche at or before sexual maturity (maturation), in females of certain mammalian species, and ceases at or near menopause (commonly considered the end of a female's reproductive life). The periodicity of menstruation gives rise to commonly used euphemisms like 'period' and 'monthly'.
Ovary	The ovary is an ovum-producing reproductive organ, often found in pairs as part of the vertebrate female reproductive system. Ovaries in female individuals are analogous to testes in male individuals, in that they are both gonads and endocrine glands.
Ovulation	Ovulation is the phase of a female's menstrual cycle in which a partially mature ovum that has yet to complete Meiosis II is released from the ovarian follicles into the oviduct. After ovulation, during the luteal phase, the egg will be available to be fertilized by sperm. Concomitantly, the uterine lining (endometrium) is thickened to be able to receive a fertilized egg.
Fall prevention	Fall prevention is a variety of actions to help reduce the number of accidental falls suffered by older people.

CHAPTER HIGHLIGHTS & NOTES: KEY TERMS, PEOPLE, PLACES, CONCEPTS

Falls and fall related injuries are among the most serious and common medical problems experienced by older adults. Nearly one-third of older persons fall each year, and half of them fall more than once.

CHAPTER QUIZ: KEY TERMS, PEOPLE, PLACES, CONCEPTS

1. In current practice, _________ is most often a synonym for female menopause. In Princeton University's online Wordnet database, _________ is listed as: •(n) _________•(n) menopause, _________, change of life (the time in a woman's life in which the menstrual cycle ends)

   The term is used for both genders by The International Menopause Society, which defines itself as 'The society for the study of all aspects of the _________ in men and women.'

   a. 1970 British Cohort Study
   b. Barry Bogin
   c. Birth order
   d. Climacteric

2. _________ is the main structural protein of the various connective tissues in animals. (The name _________ comes from the Greek kolla meaning glue and suffix -gen denoting producing). As the main component of connective tissue, it is the most abundant protein in mammals, making up from 25% to 35% of the whole-body protein content.

   a. Biological immortality
   b. Collagen
   c. Cellular senescence
   d. Centenarian

3. _________ is a progressive bone disease that is characterized by a decrease in bone mass and density which can lead to an increased risk of fracture. In _________, the bone mineral density (BMD) is reduced, bone microarchitecture deteriorates, and the amount and variety of proteins in bone are altered. _________ is defined by the World Health Organization (WHO) as a bone mineral density of 2.5 standard deviations or more below the mean peak bone mass (average of young, healthy adults) as measured by dual-energy X-ray absorptiometry; the term 'established _________' includes the presence of a fragility fracture.

   a. Osteoporosis
   b. Cataract
   c. Chronic obstructive pulmonary disease
   d. Coronary artery disease

4. A _________ is a region of repetitive nucleotide sequences at each end of a chromatid, which protects the end of the chromosome from deterioration or from fusion with neighboring chromosomes. Its name is derived from the Greek nouns telos (t????) 'end' and mer?s (μ????, root: μe?-) 'part.' _________ regions deter the degradation of genes near the ends of chromosomes by allowing chromosome ends to shorten, which necessarily occurs during chromosome replication. Without _________s, the genomes would progressively lose information and be truncated after cell division because the synthesis of Okazaki fragments requires RNA primers attaching ahead on the lagging strand.

   a. Beginning of human personhood
   b. Definitions of abortion
   c. Telomere
   d. Late termination of pregnancy

5. The _________ is a generation of people who care for their aging parents while supporting their own children.

   According to the Pew Research Center, just over 1 of every 8 Americans aged 40 to 60 is both raising a child and caring for a parent, in addition to between 7 to 10 million adults caring for their aging parents from a long distance. US Census Bureau statistics indicate that the number of older Americans aged 65 or older will double by the year 2030, to over 70 million.

   a. 1837 generation
   b. 386 Generation
   c. Baby boomer
   d. Sandwich generation

ANSWER KEY
3. Physical Changes

1. d
2. b
3. a
4. c
5. d

---

4. Longevity, Health, and Functioning

CHAPTER OUTLINE: KEY TERMS, PEOPLE, PLACES, CONCEPTS

______________	Longevity
______________	Life expectancy
______________	Quality of life
______________	Lung
______________	Coping
______________	Erectile dysfunction
______________	Cancer
______________	Lesbian
______________	Urinary incontinence
______________	Rheumatoid arthritis
______________	Arthritis
______________	Osteoarthritis

CHAPTER HIGHLIGHTS & NOTES: KEY TERMS, PEOPLE, PLACES, CONCEPTS

Longevity	The word 'longevity' is sometimes used as a synonym for 'life expectancy' in demography - however, the term 'longevity' is sometimes meant to refer only to especially long lived members of a population, whereas 'life expectancy' is always defined statistically as the average number of years remaining at a given age. For example, a population's life expectancy at birth is the same as the average age at death for all people born in the same year (in the case of cohorts). Longevity is best thought of as a term for general audiences meaning 'typical length of life' and specific statistical definitions should be clarified when necessary.
Life expectancy	Life expectancy is the expected number of years of life remaining at a given age. It is denoted by e_x , which means the average number of subsequent years of life for someone now aged x , according to a particular mortality experience.

4. Longevity, Health, and Functioning

CHAPTER HIGHLIGHTS & NOTES: KEY TERMS, PEOPLE, PLACES, CONCEPTS

Quality of life	In general, quality of life is the perceived quality of an individual's daily life, that is, an assessment of their well-being or lack thereof. This includes all emotional, social, and physical aspects of the individual's life. In health care, health-related quality of life is an assessment of how the individual's well-being may be affected over time by a disease, disability, or disorder.
Lung	Lung means wind or breath. It is a key concept in the Vajrayana traditions of Tibetan Buddhism and has a variety of meanings. Lung is a concept that's particularly important to understandings of the subtle body and the Three Vajras (body, speech and mind).
Coping	In psychology, coping is expending conscious effort to solve personal and interpersonal problems, and seeking to master, minimize or tolerate stress or conflict. Psychological coping mechanisms are commonly termed coping strategies or coping skills. Unconscious or non conscious strategies (e.g., defense mechanisms) are generally excluded.
Erectile dysfunction	Erectile dysfunction or impotence is sexual dysfunction characterized by the inability to develop or maintain an erection of the penis during sexual performance. A penile erection is the hydraulic effect of blood entering and being retained in sponge-like bodies within the penis. The process is often initiated as a result of sexual arousal, when signals are transmitted from the brain to nerves in the penis.
Cancer	Cancer , known medically as a malignant neoplasm, is a broad group of diseases involving unregulated cell growth. In cancer, cells divide and grow uncontrollably, forming malignant tumors, and invading nearby parts of the body. The cancer may also spread to more distant parts of the body through the lymphatic system or bloodstream.
Lesbian	Lesbian is the term most widely used in the English language to describe romantic or sexual attraction between women. The word may be used as a noun, to refer to women who identify themselves or who are characterized by others as having the primary attribute of female homosexuality, or as an adjective, to describe characteristics of an object or activity related to female same-sex attraction. 'Lesbian' as a concept, used to differentiate women with a shared sexual orientation, is a 20th-century construct.
Urinary incontinence	Urinary incontinence, involuntary urination, is any involuntary leakage of urine. It can be a common and distressing problem, which may have a profound impact on quality of life. Urinary incontinence almost always results from an underlying treatable medical condition but is under-reported to medical practitioners.

CHAPTER HIGHLIGHTS & NOTES: KEY TERMS, PEOPLE, PLACES, CONCEPTS

Rheumatoid arthritis	Rheumatoid arthritis is an autoimmune disease that results in a chronic, systemic inflammatory disorder that may affect many tissues and organs, but principally attacks flexible . It is widely used as an indicator of RA disease activity and response to treatment, but is not always a reliable indicator of treatment effect. The joints included in DAS28 are (bilaterally): proximal interphalangeal joints (10 joints), metacarpophalangeal joints (10), wrists (2), elbows (2), shoulders (2) and knees (2).
Arthritis	Arthritis is a form of joint disorder that involves inflammation of one or more joints. There are over 100 different forms of arthritis. The most common form, osteoarthritis is a result of trauma to the joint, infection of the joint, or age.
Osteoarthritis	Osteoarthritis also known as degenerative arthritis or degenerative joint disease or osteoarthrosis, is a group of mechanical abnormalities involving degradation of joints, including articular cartilage and subchondral bone. Symptoms may include joint pain, tenderness, stiffness, locking, and sometimes an effusion. A variety of causes--hereditary, developmental, metabolic, and mechanical deficits--may initiate processes leading to loss of cartilage.

CHAPTER QUIZ: KEY TERMS, PEOPLE, PLACES, CONCEPTS

1. The word '_________' is sometimes used as a synonym for 'life expectancy' in demography - however, the term '_________' is sometimes meant to refer only to especially long lived members of a population, whereas 'life expectancy' is always defined statistically as the average number of years remaining at a given age. For example, a population's life expectancy at birth is the same as the average age at death for all people born in the same year (in the case of cohorts). _________ is best thought of as a term for general audiences meaning 'typical length of life' and specific statistical definitions should be clarified when necessary.

   a. Biological clock
   b. British Longevity Society
   c. Calcutta Metropolitan Institute of Gerontology
   d. Longevity

2. . _________ is the expected number of years of life remaining at a given age. It is denoted by e_x, which means the average number of subsequent years of life for someone now aged x, according to a particular mortality experience. Because _________ is an average, a particular person may well die many years before or many years after their 'expected' survival.

   a. Biological clock
   b. British Longevity Society
   c. Calcutta Metropolitan Institute of Gerontology

3. _________ means wind or breath. It is a key concept in the Vajrayana traditions of Tibetan Buddhism and has a variety of meanings. _________ is a concept that's particularly important to understandings of the subtle body and the Three Vajras (body, speech and mind).

a. Lung
b. Bhakti
c. Big Mind
d. Bodymind

4. In psychology, _________ is expending conscious effort to solve personal and interpersonal problems, and seeking to master, minimize or tolerate stress or conflict.

Psychological _________ mechanisms are commonly termed _________ strategies or _________ skills. Unconscious or non conscious strategies (e.g., defense mechanisms) are generally excluded.

a. Beginning of human personhood
b. Definitions of abortion
c. Feticide
d. Coping

5. In general, _________ is the perceived quality of an individual's daily life, that is, an assessment of their well-being or lack thereof. This includes all emotional, social, and physical aspects of the individual's life. In health care, health-related _________ is an assessment of how the individual's well-being may be affected over time by a disease, disability, or disorder.

a. Cambridge Pulmonary Hypertension Outcome Review
b. Genuine progress indicator
c. Quality of life
d. Happy life expectancy

ANSWER KEY
4. Longevity, Health, and Functioning

---

1. d
2. d
3. a
4. d
5. c

---

5. Where People Live: Person—Environment Interactions

CHAPTER OUTLINE: KEY TERMS, PEOPLE, PLACES, CONCEPTS

____________	Coping
____________	Aging in place
____________	Day care
____________	Arthritis
____________	Assisted living
____________	Nursing home
____________	Baby talk
____________	Erectile dysfunction

CHAPTER HIGHLIGHTS & NOTES: KEY TERMS, PEOPLE, PLACES, CONCEPTS

Coping

In psychology, coping is expending conscious effort to solve personal and interpersonal problems, and seeking to master, minimize or tolerate stress or conflict.

Psychological coping mechanisms are commonly termed coping strategies or coping skills. Unconscious or non conscious strategies (e.g., defense mechanisms) are generally excluded.

Aging in place

The Center for Disease Control defines aging in place as 'the ability to live in one's own home and community safely, independently, and comfortably, regardless of age, income, or ability level.'

In December 2011, AARP Policy Institute and the National Conference of State Legislatures released a report entitled, 'Aging in Place: A State Survey of Livability Policies and Practices' to foster aging in place by giving state legislators examples of how laws, policies and programs can support this goal. In addition to such governmental initiatives, livability can be optimized through the incorporation of universal design principles, telecare and other assistive technologies. Assistive technologies include communications, health and wellness monitoring, home safety and security.

Day care

Child care or day care is the care of a child during the day by a person other than the child's legal guardians, typically performed by someone outside the child's immediate family. Day care is typically an ongoing service during specific periods, such as the parents' time at work.

5. Where People Live: Person—Environment Interactions

CHAPTER HIGHLIGHTS & NOTES: KEY TERMS, PEOPLE, PLACES, CONCEPTS

Arthritis	Arthritis is a form of joint disorder that involves inflammation of one or more joints. There are over 100 different forms of arthritis. The most common form, osteoarthritis is a result of trauma to the joint, infection of the joint, or age.
Assisted living	An assisted living residence or assisted living facility is a housing facility for people with disabilities. These facilities provide supervision or assistance with activities of daily living (ADLs); coordination of services by outside health care providers; and monitoring of resident activities to help to ensure their health, safety, and well-being. Assistance may include the administration or supervision of medication, or personal care services provided by a trained staff person.
Nursing home	A nursing home, convalescent home, skilled nursing facility, care home, rest home or intermediate care provides a type of residential care. They are a place of residence for people who require continual nursing care and have significant deficiencies with activities of daily living. Nursing aides and skilled nurses are usually available 24 hours a day.
Baby talk	Baby talk, also referred to as caretaker speech, infant-directed speech or child-directed speech (CDS) and informally as 'motherese', 'parentese', 'mommy talk', or 'daddy talk' is a nonstandard form of speech used by adults in talking to toddlers and infants. It is usually delivered with a 'cooing' pattern of intonation different from that of normal adult speech: high in pitch, with many glissando variations that are more pronounced than those of normal speech. It frequently displays hyperarticulation, a measure of clear speech defined by having large amounts of acoustic space between vowels as measured by formants.
Erectile dysfunction	Erectile dysfunction or impotence is sexual dysfunction characterized by the inability to develop or maintain an erection of the penis during sexual performance. A penile erection is the hydraulic effect of blood entering and being retained in sponge-like bodies within the penis. The process is often initiated as a result of sexual arousal, when signals are transmitted from the brain to nerves in the penis.

1. In psychology, _________ is expending conscious effort to solve personal and interpersonal problems, and seeking to master, minimize or tolerate stress or conflict.

   Psychological _________ mechanisms are commonly termed _________ strategies or _________ skills. Unconscious or non conscious strategies (e.g., defense mechanisms) are generally excluded.

   a. Coping
   b. Definitions of abortion
   c. Feticide
   d. Late termination of pregnancy

2. The Center for Disease Control defines _________ as 'the ability to live in one's own home and community safely, independently, and comfortably, regardless of age, income, or ability level.'

   In December 2011, AARP Policy Institute and the National Conference of State Legislatures released a report entitled, '_________: A State Survey of Livability Policies and Practices' to foster _________ by giving state legislators examples of how laws, policies and programs can support this goal. In addition to such governmental initiatives, livability can be optimized through the incorporation of universal design principles, telecare and other assistive technologies. Assistive technologies include communications, health and wellness monitoring, home safety and security.

   a. Calcutta Metropolitan Institute of Gerontology
   b. Gerontology
   c. Aging in place
   d. Definitions of abortion

3. Child care or _________ is the care of a child during the day by a person other than the child's legal guardians, typically performed by someone outside the child's immediate family. _________ is typically an ongoing service during specific periods, such as the parents' time at work.

   The service is known as child care in the United Kingdom and Australia, crèche in Ireland and New Zealand, and child care or _________ in North America (although child care also has a broader meaning).

   a. Baby bedding
   b. Day care
   c. Canadian Foundation for Children, Youth and the Law v. Canada
   d. Child care

4. . A _________, convalescent home, skilled nursing facility, care home, rest home or intermediate care provides a type of residential care. They are a place of residence for people who require continual nursing care and have significant deficiencies with activities of daily living. Nursing aides and skilled nurses are usually available 24 hours a day.

   a. Nursing home
   b. Beers Criteria

c. Berg Balance Scale
d. Bristol Activities of Daily Living Scale

5. _________ is a form of joint disorder that involves inflammation of one or more joints. There are over 100 different forms of _________. The most common form, osteo_________ is a result of trauma to the joint, infection of the joint, or age.

a. Beginning of human personhood
b. Arthritis
c. Feticide
d. Late termination of pregnancy

ANSWER KEY

5. Where People Live: Person—Environment Interactions

1. a
2. c
3. b
4. a
5. b

---

6. Attention and Memory

CHAPTER OUTLINE: KEY TERMS, PEOPLE, PLACES, CONCEPTS

- Nursing home
- Arthritis
- Baby talk
- Epilepsy
- Prophet
- Cognitive reserve
- Multilingualism
- Self-efficacy
- Telomere
- Mental health

CHAPTER HIGHLIGHTS & NOTES: KEY TERMS, PEOPLE, PLACES, CONCEPTS

Nursing home	A nursing home, convalescent home, skilled nursing facility, care home, rest home or intermediate care provides a type of residential care. They are a place of residence for people who require continual nursing care and have significant deficiencies with activities of daily living. Nursing aides and skilled nurses are usually available 24 hours a day.
Arthritis	Arthritis is a form of joint disorder that involves inflammation of one or more joints. There are over 100 different forms of arthritis. The most common form, osteoarthritis is a result of trauma to the joint, infection of the joint, or age.
Baby talk	Baby talk, also referred to as caretaker speech, infant-directed speech or child-directed speech (CDS) and informally as 'motherese', 'parentese', 'mommy talk', or 'daddy talk' is a nonstandard form of speech used by adults in talking to toddlers and infants.

It is usually delivered with a 'cooing' pattern of intonation different from that of normal adult speech: high in pitch, with many glissando variations that are more pronounced than those of normal speech. It frequently displays hyperarticulation, a measure of clear speech defined by having large amounts of acoustic space between vowels as measured by formants.

Epilepsy

Epilepsy is a common and diverse set of chronic neurological disorders characterized by seizures. It is a paroxysmal behavioral spell generally caused by an excessive disorderly discharge of cortical nerve cells of the brain and can range from clinically undetectable (electrographic seizures) to convulsions. Some definitions of epilepsy require that seizures be recurrent and unprovoked, but others require only a single seizure combined with brain alterations which increase the chance of future seizures.

Prophet

In religion, a prophet is an individual who is claimed to have been contacted by the supernatural or the divine, and to speak for them, serving as an intermediary with humanity, delivering this newfound knowledge from the supernatural entity to other people. The message that the prophet conveys is called a prophecy.

Claims of prophets have existed in many cultures through history, including Judaism, Christianity, Islam, in Ancient Greece, Zoroaster, and many others.

Cognitive reserve

The term cognitive reserve describes the mind's resistance to damage of the brain. The mind's resilience is evaluated behaviorally, whereas the neuropathological damage is evaluated histologically, although damage may be estimated using blood-based markers and imaging methods. There are two models that can be used when exploring the concept of 'reserve': brain reserve and cognitive reserve.

Multilingualism

Multilingualism is the act of using polyglotism, or using multiple languages, either by an individual speaker or by a community of speakers. Multilingual speakers outnumber monolingual speakers in the world's population. Multilingualism is becoming a social phenomenon governed by the needs of globalization and cultural openness.

Self-efficacy

Self-efficacy is the measure of the belief in one's own ability to complete tasks and reach goals. Psychologists have studied self-efficacy from several perspectives, noting various paths in the development of self-efficacy; the dynamics of self-efficacy, and lack thereof, in many different settings; interactions between self-efficacy and self-concept; and habits of attribution that contribute to, or detract from, self-efficacy.

Self-efficacy affects every area of human endeavor.

CHAPTER HIGHLIGHTS & NOTES: KEY TERMS, PEOPLE, PLACES, CONCEPTS

Telomere

A telomere is a region of repetitive nucleotide sequences at each end of a chromatid, which protects the end of the chromosome from deterioration or from fusion with neighboring chromosomes. Its name is derived from the Greek nouns telos (t????) 'end' and mer?s (μ????, root: μe?-) 'part.' Telomere regions deter the degradation of genes near the ends of chromosomes by allowing chromosome ends to shorten, which necessarily occurs during chromosome replication. Without telomeres, the genomes would progressively lose information and be truncated after cell division because the synthesis of Okazaki fragments requires RNA primers attaching ahead on the lagging strand.

Mental health

Mental health describes a level of psychological well-being, or an absence of a mental disorder. From the perspective of 'positive psychology' or 'holism', mental health may include an individual's ability to enjoy life, and create a balance between life activities and efforts to achieve psychological resilience. Mental health can also be defined as an expression of emotions, and as signifying a successful adaptation to a range of demands.

CHAPTER QUIZ: KEY TERMS, PEOPLE, PLACES, CONCEPTS

1. The term _________ describes the mind's resistance to damage of the brain. The mind's resilience is evaluated behaviorally, whereas the neuropathological damage is evaluated histologically, although damage may be estimated using blood-based markers and imaging methods. There are two models that can be used when exploring the concept of 'reserve': brain reserve and _________.

   a. Beginning of human personhood
   b. Definitions of abortion
   c. Feticide
   d. Cognitive reserve

2. . _________, also referred to as caretaker speech, infant-directed speech or child-directed speech (CDS) and informally as 'motherese', 'parentese', 'mommy talk', or 'daddy talk' is a nonstandard form of speech used by adults in talking to toddlers and infants.

   It is usually delivered with a 'cooing' pattern of intonation different from that of normal adult speech: high in pitch, with many glissando variations that are more pronounced than those of normal speech. It frequently displays hyperarticulation, a measure of clear speech defined by having large amounts of acoustic space between vowels as measured by formants.

   a. Baby furniture
   b. Baby jumping
   c. Baby on board

3. _________ is a form of joint disorder that involves inflammation of one or more joints. There are over 100 different forms of _________. The most common form, osteo_________ is a result of trauma to the joint, infection of the joint, or age.

   a. Arthritis
   b. Definitions of abortion
   c. Feticide
   d. Late termination of pregnancy

4. In religion, a _________ is an individual who is claimed to have been contacted by the supernatural or the divine, and to speak for them, serving as an intermediary with humanity, delivering this newfound knowledge from the supernatural entity to other people. The message that the _________ conveys is called a prophecy.

   Claims of _________s have existed in many cultures through history, including Judaism, Christianity, Islam, in Ancient Greece, Zoroaster, and many others.

   a. Prophet
   b. Bilocation
   c. Charism
   d. Gifts of healing

5. A _________, convalescent home, skilled nursing facility, care home, rest home or intermediate care provides a type of residential care. They are a place of residence for people who require continual nursing care and have significant deficiencies with activities of daily living. Nursing aides and skilled nurses are usually available 24 hours a day.

   a. Nursing home
   b. Beers Criteria
   c. Berg Balance Scale
   d. Bristol Activities of Daily Living Scale

ANSWER KEY
6. Attention and Memory

1. d
2. d
3. a
4. a
5. a

7. Intelligence, Reasoning, Creativity, and Wisdom

CHAPTER OUTLINE: KEY TERMS, PEOPLE, PLACES, CONCEPTS

______	Psychotherapy
______	Fluency
______	Personality
______	Arthritis
______	Lifelong learning
______	Wisdom

CHAPTER HIGHLIGHTS & NOTES: KEY TERMS, PEOPLE, PLACES, CONCEPTS

Psychotherapy	Psychotherapy is a general term referring to therapeutic interaction or treatment contracted between a trained professional and a client, patient, family, couple, or group. The problems addressed are psychological in nature and can vary in terms of their causes, influences, triggers, and potential resolutions. Accurate assessment of these and other variables is dependent on the practitioner's capability and can change or evolve as the practitioner acquires greater experience, knowledge, and insight.
Fluency	Fluency is the property of a person or of a system that delivers information quickly and with expertise.
Personality	Personality is the particular combination of emotional, attitudinal, and behavioral response patterns of an individual. Different personality theorists present their own definitions of the word based on their theoretical positions. Psychologists such as Freud, and Erik Erikson have attempted to come up with personality theories.
Arthritis	Arthritis is a form of joint disorder that involves inflammation of one or more joints. There are over 100 different forms of arthritis. The most common form, osteoarthritis is a result of trauma to the joint, infection of the joint, or age.
Lifelong learning	Lifelong learning is the 'ongoing, voluntary, and self-motivated' pursuit of knowledge for either personal or professional reasons. Therefore, it not only enhances social inclusion, active citizenship and personal development, but also competitiveness and employability.

7. Intelligence, Reasoning, Creativity, and Wisdom

CHAPTER HIGHLIGHTS & NOTES: KEY TERMS, PEOPLE, PLACES, CONCEPTS

Wisdom	Wisdom has, in the Western tradition, been listed as one of four cardinal virtues. As a virtue it is a habit or disposition to perform the action with the highest degree of adequacy under any given circumstance. This implies a possession or seeking of knowledge of the given circumstances.

CHAPTER QUIZ: KEY TERMS, PEOPLE, PLACES, CONCEPTS

1. _________ is the property of a person or of a system that delivers information quickly and with expertise.

 a. Fluency
 b. Code-mixing
 c. Cohort model
 d. Collaborative model

2. _________ is a general term referring to therapeutic interaction or treatment contracted between a trained professional and a client, patient, family, couple, or group. The problems addressed are psychological in nature and can vary in terms of their causes, influences, triggers, and potential resolutions. Accurate assessment of these and other variables is dependent on the practitioner's capability and can change or evolve as the practitioner acquires greater experience, knowledge, and insight.

 a. Behavioral psychotherapy
 b. Psychotherapy
 c. Brad Lamm
 d. Brief psychotherapy

3. _________ is the particular combination of emotional, attitudinal, and behavioral response patterns of an individual. Different _________ theorists present their own definitions of the word based on their theoretical positions. Psychologists such as Freud, and Erik Erikson have attempted to come up with _________ theories.

 a. 1970 British Cohort Study
 b. Barry Bogin
 c. Birth order
 d. Personality

4. . _________ is a form of joint disorder that involves inflammation of one or more joints. There are over 100 different forms of _________. The most common form, osteo_________ is a result of trauma to the joint, infection of the joint, or age.

 a. Beginning of human personhood
 b. Arthritis
 c. Feticide

5. _________ is the 'ongoing, voluntary, and self-motivated' pursuit of knowledge for either personal or professional reasons. Therefore, it not only enhances social inclusion, active citizenship and personal development, but also competitiveness and employability.

Evolved from the term "life-long learners" created by Leslie Watkins and used by Professor Clint Taylor (CSULA) and Superintendent for the Temple City Unified School District's mission statement in 1993, the term recognizes that learning is not confined to childhood or the classroom but takes place throughout life and in a range of situations.

a. Lifelong learning
b. Grundtvig programme
c. Beginning of human personhood
d. Definitions of abortion

ANSWER KEY
7. Intelligence, Reasoning, Creativity, and Wisdom

---

1. a
2. b
3. d
4. b
5. a

---

8. Social Cognition

CHAPTER OUTLINE: KEY TERMS, PEOPLE, PLACES, CONCEPTS

________	Young adult
________	Personality
________	Cognitive reserve
________	Coping
________	Arthritis
________	Self-esteem

CHAPTER HIGHLIGHTS & NOTES: KEY TERMS, PEOPLE, PLACES, CONCEPTS

Young adult	A young/prime adult, according to Erik Erikson's stages of human development, is generally a person in the age range of 20 to 40, whereas an adolescent is a person aging from 13 to 19, although definitions and opinions vary. The young adult stage in human development precedes middle adulthood. A person in the middle adulthood stage ages from 40 to 64. In old age, a person is 65 years old or older.
Personality	Personality is the particular combination of emotional, attitudinal, and behavioral response patterns of an individual. Different personality theorists present their own definitions of the word based on their theoretical positions. Psychologists such as Freud, and Erik Erikson have attempted to come up with personality theories.
Cognitive reserve	The term cognitive reserve describes the mind's resistance to damage of the brain. The mind's resilience is evaluated behaviorally, whereas the neuropathological damage is evaluated histologically, although damage may be estimated using blood-based markers and imaging methods. There are two models that can be used when exploring the concept of 'reserve': brain reserve and cognitive reserve.
Coping	In psychology, coping is expending conscious effort to solve personal and interpersonal problems, and seeking to master, minimize or tolerate stress or conflict. Psychological coping mechanisms are commonly termed coping strategies or coping skills. Unconscious or non conscious strategies (e.g., defense mechanisms) are generally excluded.

8. Social Cognition

CHAPTER HIGHLIGHTS & NOTES: KEY TERMS, PEOPLE, PLACES, CONCEPTS

Arthritis	Arthritis is a form of joint disorder that involves inflammation of one or more joints. There are over 100 different forms of arthritis. The most common form, osteoarthritis is a result of trauma to the joint, infection of the joint, or age.
Self-esteem	Self-esteem is a term used in psychology to reflect person's overall emotional evaluation of his or her own worth. It is a judgment of oneself as well as an attitude toward the self. Self-esteem encompasses beliefs (for example, 'I am competent,' 'I am worthy') and emotions such as triumph, despair, pride and shame.

CHAPTER QUIZ: KEY TERMS, PEOPLE, PLACES, CONCEPTS

1. _________ is a form of joint disorder that involves inflammation of one or more joints. There are over 100 different forms of _________. The most common form, osteo_________ is a result of trauma to the joint, infection of the joint, or age.

   a. Beginning of human personhood
   b. Definitions of abortion
   c. Arthritis
   d. Late termination of pregnancy

2. A young/prime adult, according to Erik Erikson's stages of human development, is generally a person in the age range of 20 to 40, whereas an adolescent is a person aging from 13 to 19, although definitions and opinions vary. The _________ stage in human development precedes middle adulthood. A person in the middle adulthood stage ages from 40 to 64. In old age, a person is 65 years old or older.

   a. 1970 British Cohort Study
   b. Young adult
   c. Birth order
   d. Casa viva

3. The term _________ describes the mind's resistance to damage of the brain. The mind's resilience is evaluated behaviorally, whereas the neuropathological damage is evaluated histologically, although damage may be estimated using blood-based markers and imaging methods. There are two models that can be used when exploring the concept of 'reserve': brain reserve and _________.

   a. Beginning of human personhood
   b. Cognitive reserve
   c. Feticide
   d. Late termination of pregnancy

4. . _________ is the particular combination of emotional, attitudinal, and behavioral response patterns of an individual.

Different _________ theorists present their own definitions of the word based on their theoretical positions. Psychologists such as Freud, and Erik Erikson have attempted to come up with _________ theories.

a. 1970 British Cohort Study
b. Barry Bogin
c. Personality
d. Casa viva

5. In psychology, _________ is expending conscious effort to solve personal and interpersonal problems, and seeking to master, minimize or tolerate stress or conflict.

Psychological _________ mechanisms are commonly termed _________ strategies or _________ skills. Unconscious or non conscious strategies (e.g., defense mechanisms) are generally excluded.

a. Beginning of human personhood
b. Definitions of abortion
c. Feticide
d. Coping

ANSWER KEY
8. Social Cognition

1. c
2. b
3. b
4. c
5. d

9. Personality

CHAPTER OUTLINE: KEY TERMS, PEOPLE, PLACES, CONCEPTS

_______________ Personality

_______________ Erectile dysfunction

_______________ Personality development

_______________ Midlife crisis

_______________ Subjective well-being

_______________ Arthritis

CHAPTER HIGHLIGHTS & NOTES: KEY TERMS, PEOPLE, PLACES, CONCEPTS

Personality

Personality is the particular combination of emotional, attitudinal, and behavioral response patterns of an individual. Different personality theorists present their own definitions of the word based on their theoretical positions. Psychologists such as Freud, and Erik Erikson have attempted to come up with personality theories.

Erectile dysfunction

Erectile dysfunction or impotence is sexual dysfunction characterized by the inability to develop or maintain an erection of the penis during sexual performance.

A penile erection is the hydraulic effect of blood entering and being retained in sponge-like bodies within the penis. The process is often initiated as a result of sexual arousal, when signals are transmitted from the brain to nerves in the penis.

Personality development

An individual's personality is an aggregate conglomeration of the decisions they have made throughout their life and the memory of the experiences to which these decisions led. There are inherent natural, genetic, and environmental factors that contribute to the development of our personality. According to process of socialization, 'personality also colors our values, beliefs, and expectations ... Hereditary factors that contribute to personality development do so as a result of interactions with the particular social environment in which people live.' There are several personality types as Katharine Cook Briggs and Isabel Briggs Myers illustrated in several personalities typology tests, which are based on Carl Jung's school of Analytical psychology.

Midlife crisis

Midlife crisis is a term coined in 1965 by Elliott Jaques stating a time where adults come to realize their own mortality and how much time is left in their life.

9. Personality

CHAPTER HIGHLIGHTS & NOTES: KEY TERMS, PEOPLE, PLACES, CONCEPTS

	A midlife crisis is experienced by many people during the midlife transition when they realize that life may be more than halfway over. Sometimes, a crisis can be triggered by transitions experienced in these years, such as andropause or menopause, the death of parents or other causes of grief, unemployment or underemployment, realizing that a job or career is hated but not knowing how else to earn an equivalent living, or children leaving home.
Subjective well-being	Subjective well-being refers to how people experience the quality of their lives and includes both emotional reactions and cognitive judgments. Psychologists have defined happiness as a combination of life satisfaction and the relative frequency of positive and negative affect. Subjective well being therefore encompasses moods and emotions as well as evaluations of one's satisfaction with general and specific areas of one's life.
Arthritis	Arthritis is a form of joint disorder that involves inflammation of one or more joints. There are over 100 different forms of arthritis. The most common form, osteoarthritis is a result of trauma to the joint, infection of the joint, or age.

CHAPTER QUIZ: KEY TERMS, PEOPLE, PLACES, CONCEPTS

1. _________ is the particular combination of emotional, attitudinal, and behavioral response patterns of an individual. Different _________ theorists present their own definitions of the word based on their theoretical positions. Psychologists such as Freud, and Erik Erikson have attempted to come up with _________ theories.

   a. 1970 British Cohort Study
   b. Barry Bogin
   c. Birth order
   d. Personality

2. _________ or impotence is sexual dysfunction characterized by the inability to develop or maintain an erection of the penis during sexual performance.

   A penile erection is the hydraulic effect of blood entering and being retained in sponge-like bodies within the penis. The process is often initiated as a result of sexual arousal, when signals are transmitted from the brain to nerves in the penis.

   a. Beginning of human personhood
   b. Definitions of abortion
   c. Feticide
   d. Erectile dysfunction

3. An individual's personality is an aggregate conglomeration of the decisions they have made throughout their life and the memory of the experiences to which these decisions led. There are inherent natural, genetic, and environmental factors that contribute to the development of our personality. According to process of socialization, 'personality also colors our values, beliefs, and expectations ... Hereditary factors that contribute to _________ do so as a result of interactions with the particular social environment in which people live.' There are several personality types as Katharine Cook Briggs and Isabel Briggs Myers illustrated in several personalities typology tests, which are based on Carl Jung's school of Analytical psychology.

   a. Breakthrough Collaborative
   b. Career
   c. Career assessment
   d. Personality development

4. _________ is a term coined in 1965 by Elliott Jaques stating a time where adults come to realize their own mortality and how much time is left in their life. A _________ is experienced by many people during the midlife transition when they realize that life may be more than halfway over. Sometimes, a crisis can be triggered by transitions experienced in these years, such as andropause or menopause, the death of parents or other causes of grief, unemployment or underemployment, realizing that a job or career is hated but not knowing how else to earn an equivalent living, or children leaving home.

   a. Beginning of human personhood
   b. Midlife crisis
   c. Feticide
   d. Late termination of pregnancy

5. _________ refers to how people experience the quality of their lives and includes both emotional reactions and cognitive judgments. Psychologists have defined happiness as a combination of life satisfaction and the relative frequency of positive and negative affect. Subjective well being therefore encompasses moods and emotions as well as evaluations of one's satisfaction with general and specific areas of one's life.

   a. Subjective well-being
   b. Hedonic treadmill
   c. Joie de vivre
   d. Peak experience

ANSWER KEY
9. Personality

---

1. d
2. d
3. d
4. b
5. a

---

10. Clinical Assessment, Mental Health, and Mental Disorders

CHAPTER OUTLINE: KEY TERMS, PEOPLE, PLACES, CONCEPTS

- ______ Mental health
- ______ Coping
- ______ Brain-derived neurotrophic factor
- ______ Geriatrics
- ______ Geriatric Depression Scale
- ______ Cognitive reserve
- ______ Psychotherapy
- ______ Delirium
- ______ Dementia
- ______ Personality
- ______ Donepezil
- ______ Galantamine
- ______ Memantine
- ______ Rivastigmine
- ______ Stroke
- ______ Vascular dementia
- ______ Lesbian
- ______ Arthritis

Mental health	Mental health describes a level of psychological well-being, or an absence of a mental disorder. From the perspective of 'positive psychology' or 'holism', mental health may include an individual's ability to enjoy life, and create a balance between life activities and efforts to achieve psychological resilience. Mental health can also be defined as an expression of emotions, and as signifying a successful adaptation to a range of demands.
Coping	In psychology, coping is expending conscious effort to solve personal and interpersonal problems, and seeking to master, minimize or tolerate stress or conflict. Psychological coping mechanisms are commonly termed coping strategies or coping skills. Unconscious or non conscious strategies (e.g., defense mechanisms) are generally excluded.
Brain-derived neurotrophic factor	Brain-derived neurotrophic factor, also known as Brain derived neurotrophic factor, is a secreted protein that, in humans, is encoded by the Brain derived neurotrophic factor gene. Brain derived neurotrophic factor is a member of the 'neurotrophin' family of growth factors, which are related to the canonical 'nerve growth factor', NGF. Neurotrophic factors are found in the brain and the periphery.
Geriatrics	Geriatrics or geriatric medicine is a sub-specialty of internal medicine and family medicine that focuses on health care of elderly people. It aims to promote health by preventing and treating diseases and disabilities in older adults. There is no set age at which patients may be under the care of a geriatrician or geriatric physician, a physician who specializes in the care of elderly people.
Geriatric Depression Scale	The Geriatric Depression Scale is a 30-item self-report assessment used to identify depression in the elderly. The scale was first developed in 1982 by J.A. Yesavage and others.
Cognitive reserve	The term cognitive reserve describes the mind's resistance to damage of the brain. The mind's resilience is evaluated behaviorally, whereas the neuropathological damage is evaluated histologically, although damage may be estimated using blood-based markers and imaging methods. There are two models that can be used when exploring the concept of 'reserve': brain reserve and cognitive reserve.
Psychotherapy	Psychotherapy is a general term referring to therapeutic interaction or treatment contracted between a trained professional and a client, patient, family, couple, or group. The problems addressed are psychological in nature and can vary in terms of their causes, influences, triggers, and potential resolutions. Accurate assessment of these and other variables is dependent on the practitioner's capability and can change or evolve as the practitioner acquires greater experience, knowledge, and insight.
Delirium	Delirium, or acute confusional state, is a syndrome that presents as severe confusion and disorientation, developing with relatively rapid onset and fluctuating in intensity.

It is a syndrome which occurs more frequently in people in their later years. Delirium represents an organically caused decline from a previously attained baseline level of cognitive function.

Dementia

Dementia is a serious loss of global cognitive ability in a previously unimpaired person, beyond what might be expected from normal aging. It may be static, the result of a unique global brain injury, or progressive, resulting in long-term decline due to damage or disease in the body. Although dementia is far more common in the geriatric population (about 5% of those over 65 are said to be involved), it can occur before the age of 65, in which case it is termed 'early onset dementia'.

Personality

Personality is the particular combination of emotional, attitudinal, and behavioral response patterns of an individual. Different personality theorists present their own definitions of the word based on their theoretical positions. Psychologists such as Freud, and Erik Erikson have attempted to come up with personality theories.

Donepezil

Donepezil, marketed under the trade name Aricept by its developer Eisai and partner Pfizer, and also marketed under the brand name DONEP by Alkem Pentacare, is a centrally acting reversible acetylcholinesterase inhibitor. Its main therapeutic use is in the palliative treatment of Alzheimer's disease. Common side effects include gastrointestinal upset.

Galantamine

Galantamine is used for the treatment of mild to moderate Alzheimer's disease and various other memory impairments, in particular those of vascular origin. It is an alkaloid that is obtained synthetically or from the bulbs and flowers of Galanthus caucasicus (Caucasian snowdrop, Voronov's snowdrop), Galanthus woronowii (Amaryllidaceae) and related genera like Narcissus (daffodil)), Leucojum (snowflake), and Lycoris including Lycoris radiata (Red Spider Lily).

Studies of usage in modern medicine began in the Soviet Union in the 1950s.

Memantine

Memantine is the first in a novel class of Alzheimer's disease medications acting on the glutamatergic system by blocking NMDA-type glutamate receptors. It was first synthesized by Eli Lilly and Company in 1968. Memantine is marketed under the brands Axura and Akatinol by Merz, Namenda by Forest, Ebixa and Abixa by Lundbeck and Memox by Unipharm. Memantine has been shown to have a modest effect in moderate-to-severe Alzheimer's disease and in dementia with Lewy bodies.

Rivastigmine

Rivastigmine is a parasympathomimetic or cholinergic agent for the treatment of mild to moderate dementia of the Alzheimer's type and dementia due to Parkinson's disease. The drug can be administered orally or via a transdermal patch; the latter form reduces the prevalence of side effects, which typically include nausea and vomiting. The drug is eliminated through the urine, and appears to have relatively few drug-drug interactions.

Stroke

A stroke, sometimes referred to as a cerebrovascular accident, is the rapid loss of brain function due to disturbance in the blood supply to the brain. This can be due to ischemia (lack of blood flow) caused by blockage (thrombosis, arterial embolism), or a hemorrhage. As a result, the affected area of the brain cannot function, which might result in an inability to move one or more limbs on one side of the body, inability to understand or formulate speech, or an inability to see one side of the visual field.

Vascular dementia

Vascular dementia or 'multi-infarct dementia' is dementia caused by problems in supply of blood to the brain, typically by a series of minor strokes. This type of dementia was previously referred to as 'multi-infarct dementia', and also hardening of the arteries. Vascular dementia is the second most common form of dementia after Alzheimer's disease (AD) in older adults.

Lesbian

Lesbian is the term most widely used in the English language to describe romantic or sexual attraction between women. The word may be used as a noun, to refer to women who identify themselves or who are characterized by others as having the primary attribute of female homosexuality, or as an adjective, to describe characteristics of an object or activity related to female same-sex attraction.

'Lesbian' as a concept, used to differentiate women with a shared sexual orientation, is a 20th-century construct.

Arthritis

Arthritis is a form of joint disorder that involves inflammation of one or more joints. There are over 100 different forms of arthritis. The most common form, osteoarthritis is a result of trauma to the joint, infection of the joint, or age.

CHAPTER QUIZ: KEY TERMS, PEOPLE, PLACES, CONCEPTS

1. The _________ is a 30-item self-report assessment used to identify depression in the elderly. The scale was first developed in 1982 by J.A. Yesavage and others.

   a. Cognitive reserve
   b. Geriatric Depression Scale
   c. Beginning of human personhood
   d. Definitions of abortion

2. . _________ or _________(s) medicine is a sub-specialty of internal medicine and family medicine that focuses on health care of elderly people. It aims to promote health by preventing and treating diseases and disabilities in older adults. There is no set age at which patients may be under the care of a geriatrician or _________(s) physician, a physician who specializes in the care of elderly people.

a. Beginning of human personhood
b. Definitions of abortion
c. Geriatrics
d. Late termination of pregnancy

3. _________, or acute confusional state, is a syndrome that presents as severe confusion and disorientation, developing with relatively rapid onset and fluctuating in intensity. It is a syndrome which occurs more frequently in people in their later years. _________ represents an organically caused decline from a previously attained baseline level of cognitive function.

a. Cerebellar cognitive affective syndrome
b. Clinical Dementia Rating
c. Delirium
d. Cognitive remediation

4. _________ describes a level of psychological well-being, or an absence of a mental disorder. From the perspective of 'positive psychology' or 'holism', _________ may include an individual's ability to enjoy life, and create a balance between life activities and efforts to achieve psychological resilience. _________ can also be defined as an expression of emotions, and as signifying a successful adaptation to a range of demands.

a. Born This Way Foundation
b. Broaden-and-build
c. Character orientation
d. Mental health

5. The term _________ describes the mind's resistance to damage of the brain. The mind's resilience is evaluated behaviorally, whereas the neuropathological damage is evaluated histologically, although damage may be estimated using blood-based markers and imaging methods. There are two models that can be used when exploring the concept of 'reserve': brain reserve and _________.

a. Cognitive reserve
b. Definitions of abortion
c. Feticide
d. Late termination of pregnancy

ANSWER KEY
10. Clinical Assessment, Mental Health, and Mental Disorders

---

1. b
2. c
3. c
4. d
5. a

---

11. Relationships

CHAPTER OUTLINE: KEY TERMS, PEOPLE, PLACES, CONCEPTS

- Assortative mating
- Casual sex
- Falling in love
- Rivastigmine
- Elder abuse
- Adolescence
- Lesbian
- Arthritis
- Personality
- Parenting
- Single parent
- Sandwich generation
- Adoption

11. Relationships

CHAPTER HIGHLIGHTS & NOTES: KEY TERMS, PEOPLE, PLACES, CONCEPTS

Assortative mating	Assortative mating is a nonrandom mating pattern in which individuals with similar genotypes and/or phenotypes mate with one another more frequently than what would be expected under a random mating pattern. For example, it is common for individuals of similar body size to mate with one another. Less commonly, in negative assortative mating individuals with diverse traits mate more frequently than what would be expected in random mating.
Casual sex	Casual sex or hooking up are certain types of human sexual activity outside the context of a romantic relationship. The term is not always used consistently: it may refer to extramarital sex, sex in a casual relationship, one-time encounters, promiscuous sex, or sex in the absence of emotional attachment or love, which can include prostitution and swinging. Other terms sometimes associated with casual sex include recreational sex, social sex, nonrelationship sex, no-strings-attached (NSA) sex, physical relationship, or sex with no games.
Falling in love	In romantic relationships, falling in love is mainly a Western concept of moving from a feeling of neutrality towards a person to one of love. The term is generally used to describe an (eventual) love that is strong.
Rivastigmine	Rivastigmine is a parasympathomimetic or cholinergic agent for the treatment of mild to moderate dementia of the Alzheimer's type and dementia due to Parkinson's disease. The drug can be administered orally or via a transdermal patch; the latter form reduces the prevalence of side effects, which typically include nausea and vomiting. The drug is eliminated through the urine, and appears to have relatively few drug-drug interactions.
Elder abuse	Elder abuse is 'a single, or repeated act, or lack of appropriate action, occurring within any relationship where there is an expectation of trust, which causes harm or distress to an older person.' This definition has been adopted by the World Health Organization from a definition put forward by Action on Elder Abuse in the UK. Laws protecting the elderly from abuse are similar to, and related to, laws protecting dependent adults from abuse. The core element to the harm of elder abuse is the 'expectation of trust' of the older person toward their abuser. Thus, it includes harms by people the older person knows or with whom they have a relationship, such as a spouse, partner or family member, a friend or neighbor, or people that the older person relies on for services.
Adolescence	Adolescence is a transitional stage of physical and psychological human development that generally occurs during the period from puberty to legal adulthood (age of majority). The period of adolescence is most closely associated with the teenage years, though its physical, psychological and cultural expressions may begin earlier and end later.

Lesbian	Lesbian is the term most widely used in the English language to describe romantic or sexual attraction between women. The word may be used as a noun, to refer to women who identify themselves or who are characterized by others as having the primary attribute of female homosexuality, or as an adjective, to describe characteristics of an object or activity related to female same-sex attraction. 'Lesbian' as a concept, used to differentiate women with a shared sexual orientation, is a 20th-century construct.
Arthritis	Arthritis is a form of joint disorder that involves inflammation of one or more joints. There are over 100 different forms of arthritis. The most common form, osteoarthritis is a result of trauma to the joint, infection of the joint, or age.
Personality	Personality is the particular combination of emotional, attitudinal, and behavioral response patterns of an individual. Different personality theorists present their own definitions of the word based on their theoretical positions. Psychologists such as Freud, and Erik Erikson have attempted to come up with personality theories.
Parenting	Parenting is the process of promoting and supporting the physical, emotional, social, and intellectual development of a child from infancy to adulthood. Parenting refers to the aspects of raising a child aside from the biological relationship. The most common partaker in parenting is the biological parent(s) of the child in question, although others may be an older sibling, a grand-parent, a legal guardian, aunt, uncle or other family member or a family friend.
Single parent	A single parent is a parent, not living with a spouse or partner, who has most of the day-to-day responsibilities in raising the child or children. A single parent is usually considered the primary caregiver, meaning the parent the children have residency with the majority of the time. If the parents are separated or divorced, children live with their custodial parent and have visitation or secondary residence with their noncustodial parent.
Sandwich generation	The Sandwich generation is a generation of people who care for their aging parents while supporting their own children. According to the Pew Research Center, just over 1 of every 8 Americans aged 40 to 60 is both raising a child and caring for a parent, in addition to between 7 to 10 million adults caring for their aging parents from a long distance. US Census Bureau statistics indicate that the number of older Americans aged 65 or older will double by the year 2030, to over 70 million.

11. Relationships

CHAPTER HIGHLIGHTS & NOTES: KEY TERMS, PEOPLE, PLACES, CONCEPTS

Adoption	Adoption is a process whereby a person assumes the parenting for another and, in so doing, permanently transfers all rights and responsibilities, along with filiation, from the biological parent or parents. Unlike guardianship or other systems designed for the care of the young, adoption is intended to effect a permanent change in status and as such requires societal recognition, either through legal or religious sanction. Historically, some societies have enacted specific laws governing adoption; where others have tried to achieve adoption through less formal means, notably via contracts that specified inheritance rights and parental responsibilities without an accompanying transfer of filiation.

CHAPTER QUIZ: KEY TERMS, PEOPLE, PLACES, CONCEPTS

1. _________ is a transitional stage of physical and psychological human development that generally occurs during the period from puberty to legal adulthood (age of majority). The period of _________ is most closely associated with the teenage years, though its physical, psychological and cultural expressions may begin earlier and end later. For example, although puberty has been historically associated with the onset of adolescent development, it now typically begins prior to the teenage years and there has been a normative shift of it occurring in pre_________, particularly in females .

   a. Closed adoption
   b. Deinstitutionalisation
   c. Adolescence
   d. Foundling hospital

2. _________ is 'a single, or repeated act, or lack of appropriate action, occurring within any relationship where there is an expectation of trust, which causes harm or distress to an older person.' This definition has been adopted by the World Health Organization from a definition put forward by Action on _________ in the UK. Laws protecting the elderly from abuse are similar to, and related to, laws protecting dependent adults from abuse.

   The core element to the harm of _________ is the 'expectation of trust' of the older person toward their abuser. Thus, it includes harms by people the older person knows or with whom they have a relationship, such as a spouse, partner or family member, a friend or neighbor, or people that the older person relies on for services.

   a. Biological clock
   b. British Longevity Society
   c. Calcutta Metropolitan Institute of Gerontology
   d. Elder abuse

3. . _________ is a nonrandom mating pattern in which individuals with similar genotypes and/or phenotypes mate with one another more frequently than what would be expected under a random mating pattern. For example, it is common for individuals of similar body size to mate with one another.

Less commonly, in negative _________ individuals with diverse traits mate more frequently than what would be expected in random mating.

a. Assortative mating
b. Beginning of human personhood
c. Definitions of abortion
d. Feticide

4. _________ or hooking up are certain types of human sexual activity outside the context of a romantic relationship. The term is not always used consistently: it may refer to extramarital sex, sex in a casual relationship, one-time encounters, promiscuous sex, or sex in the absence of emotional attachment or love, which can include prostitution and swinging.

Other terms sometimes associated with _________ include recreational sex, social sex, nonrelationship sex, no-strings-attached (NSA) sex, physical relationship, or sex with no games.

a. Beginning of human personhood
b. Definitions of abortion
c. Feticide
d. Casual sex

5. In romantic relationships, _________ is mainly a Western concept of moving from a feeling of neutrality towards a person to one of love. The term is generally used to describe an (eventual) love that is strong.

a. Biological basis of love
b. Breakup
c. Broken heart
d. Falling in love

ANSWER KEY
11. Relationships

---

1. c
2. d
3. a
4. d
5. d

---

12. Work, Leisure, and Retirement

CHAPTER OUTLINE: KEY TERMS, PEOPLE, PLACES, CONCEPTS

______	Prophet
______	Self-efficacy
______	Wisdom
______	Lesbian
______	Leadership
______	Sexual harassment
______	Retirement

CHAPTER HIGHLIGHTS & NOTES: KEY TERMS, PEOPLE, PLACES, CONCEPTS

Prophet	In religion, a prophet is an individual who is claimed to have been contacted by the supernatural or the divine, and to speak for them, serving as an intermediary with humanity, delivering this newfound knowledge from the supernatural entity to other people. The message that the prophet conveys is called a prophecy. Claims of prophets have existed in many cultures through history, including Judaism, Christianity, Islam, in Ancient Greece, Zoroaster, and many others.
Self-efficacy	Self-efficacy is the measure of the belief in one's own ability to complete tasks and reach goals. Psychologists have studied self-efficacy from several perspectives, noting various paths in the development of self-efficacy; the dynamics of self-efficacy, and lack thereof, in many different settings; interactions between self-efficacy and self-concept; and habits of attribution that contribute to, or detract from, self-efficacy. Self-efficacy affects every area of human endeavor.
Wisdom	Wisdom has, in the Western tradition, been listed as one of four cardinal virtues. As a virtue it is a habit or disposition to perform the action with the highest degree of adequacy under any given circumstance. This implies a possession or seeking of knowledge of the given circumstances.

Lesbian	Lesbian is the term most widely used in the English language to describe romantic or sexual attraction between women. The word may be used as a noun, to refer to women who identify themselves or who are characterized by others as having the primary attribute of female homosexuality, or as an adjective, to describe characteristics of an object or activity related to female same-sex attraction. 'Lesbian' as a concept, used to differentiate women with a shared sexual orientation, is a 20th-century construct.
Leadership	Leadership has been described as 'a process of social influence in which one person can enlist the aid and support of others in the accomplishment of a common task', although there are alternative definitions of leadership. For example, some understand a leader simply as somebody whom people follow, or as somebody who guides or directs others, while others define leadership as 'organizing a group of people to achieve a common goal'. Studies of leadership have produced theories involving traits, situational interaction, function, behavior, power, vision and values, charisma, and intelligence, among others.
Sexual harassment	Sexual harassment is bullying or coercion of a sexual nature, or the unwelcome or inappropriate promise of rewards in exchange for sexual favors. In most modern legal contexts, sexual harassment is illegal. As defined by the US EEOC, 'It is unlawful to harass a person (an applicant or employee) because of that person's sex.' Harassment can include 'sexual harassment' or unwelcome sexual advances, requests for sexual favors, and other verbal or physical harassment of a sexual nature.
Retirement	Retirement is the point where a person stops employment completely. A person may also semi-retire by reducing work hours. Many people choose to retire when they are eligible for private or public pension benefits, although some are forced to retire when physical conditions no longer allow the person to work any more (by illness or accident) or as a result of legislation concerning their position.

12. Work, Leisure, and Retirement

CHAPTER QUIZ: KEY TERMS, PEOPLE, PLACES, CONCEPTS

1. _________ has been described as 'a process of social influence in which one person can enlist the aid and support of others in the accomplishment of a common task', although there are alternative definitions of _________. For example, some understand a leader simply as somebody whom people follow, or as somebody who guides or directs others, while others define _________ as 'organizing a group of people to achieve a common goal'.

   Studies of _________ have produced theories involving traits, situational interaction, function, behavior, power, vision and values, charisma, and intelligence, among others.

   a. Born This Way Foundation
   b. Leadership
   c. Character orientation
   d. Confidence

2. _________ is the measure of the belief in one's own ability to complete tasks and reach goals. Psychologists have studied _________ from several perspectives, noting various paths in the development of _________; the dynamics of _________, and lack thereof, in many different settings; interactions between _________ and self-concept; and habits of attribution that contribute to, or detract from, _________.

   _________ affects every area of human endeavor.

   a. Born This Way Foundation
   b. Self-efficacy
   c. Character orientation
   d. Confidence

3. _________ is bullying or coercion of a sexual nature, or the unwelcome or inappropriate promise of rewards in exchange for sexual favors. In most modern legal contexts, _________ is illegal. As defined by the US EEOC, 'It is unlawful to harass a person (an applicant or employee) because of that person's sex.' Harassment can include '_________' or unwelcome sexual advances, requests for sexual favors, and other verbal or physical harassment of a sexual nature.

   a. Sexual harassment
   b. Feminist sexology
   c. Feminist views on sexuality
   d. Lipstick feminism

4. . _________ is the term most widely used in the English language to describe romantic or sexual attraction between women. The word may be used as a noun, to refer to women who identify themselves or who are characterized by others as having the primary attribute of female homosexuality, or as an adjective, to describe characteristics of an object or activity related to female same-sex attraction.

   '_________' as a concept, used to differentiate women with a shared sexual orientation, is a 20th-century construct.

   a. Banjee

b. Lesbian
c. Heteroflexibility
d. Heterophile

5. In religion, a _________ is an individual who is claimed to have been contacted by the supernatural or the divine, and to speak for them, serving as an intermediary with humanity, delivering this newfound knowledge from the supernatural entity to other people. The message that the _________ conveys is called a prophecy.

   Claims of _________s have existed in many cultures through history, including Judaism, Christianity, Islam, in Ancient Greece, Zoroaster, and many others.

   a. Barakah
   b. Prophet
   c. Charism
   d. Gifts of healing

ANSWER KEY

12. Work, Leisure, and Retirement

---

1. b

2. b

3. a

4. b

5. b

---

13. Dying and Bereavement

CHAPTER OUTLINE: KEY TERMS, PEOPLE, PLACES, CONCEPTS

- Thanatology
- Grief
- Clinical death
- Erectile dysfunction
- Euthanasia
- Assisted suicide
- Successful aging
- Suicide
- Personality
- Death anxiety
- Terror management theory
- Memorial service
- Lesbian
- Anticipatory grief
- Coping

13. Dying and Bereavement

Thanatology	Thanatology is the scientific study of death. It investigates the mechanisms and forensic aspects of death, such as bodily changes that accompany death and the post-mortem period, as well as wider social aspects related to death. It is primarily an interdisciplinary study offered as a course of study at numerous colleges and universities.
Grief	Grief is a multifaceted response to loss, particularly to the loss of someone or something to which a bond was formed. Although conventionally focused on the emotional response to loss, it also has physical, cognitive, behavioral, social, spiritual, and philosophical dimensions. While the terms are often used interchangeably, bereavement refers to the state of loss, and grief is the reaction to loss.
Clinical death	Clinical death is the medical term for cessation of blood circulation and breathing, the two necessary criteria to sustain human and many other organisms' lives. It occurs when the heart stops beating in a regular rhythm, a condition called cardiac arrest. The term is also sometimes used in resuscitation research.
Erectile dysfunction	Erectile dysfunction or impotence is sexual dysfunction characterized by the inability to develop or maintain an erection of the penis during sexual performance. A penile erection is the hydraulic effect of blood entering and being retained in sponge-like bodies within the penis. The process is often initiated as a result of sexual arousal, when signals are transmitted from the brain to nerves in the penis.
Euthanasia	Euthanasia refers to the practice of intentionally ending a life in order to relieve pain and suffering. There are different euthanasia laws in each country. The British House of Lords Select Committee on Medical Ethics defines euthanasia as 'a deliberate intervention undertaken with the express intention of ending a life, to relieve intractable suffering'.
Assisted suicide	Assisted suicide is a general term for a suicide committed by someone with assistance from another person or persons. It is often confused with euthanasia (sometimes called 'mercy killing'), in that euthanasia refers to the killing of another in order to relieve dire suffering, and physician aid in dying, which is a practice in which a physician provides a competent, terminally ill patient with a prescription for a lethal dose of medication, upon the patient's request, which the patient intends to use to end his or her own life. Discussion of assisted suicide centers on legal, religious, and moral conceptions of suicide and a personal 'right to death'.
Successful aging	Successful aging or successful ageing (British English) refers to physical, mental and social well-being in older age. The concept of successful aging can be traced back to the 1950s, and was popularized in the 1980s.

13. Dying and Bereavement

CHAPTER HIGHLIGHTS & NOTES: KEY TERMS, PEOPLE, PLACES, CONCEPTS

Suicide	Suicide is the act of intentionally causing one's own death. Suicide is often committed out of despair, the cause of which is frequently attributed to a mental disorder such as depression, bipolar disorder, schizophrenia, borderline personality disorder, alcoholism, or drug abuse. Stress factors such as financial difficulties or troubles with interpersonal relationships often play a role.
Personality	Personality is the particular combination of emotional, attitudinal, and behavioral response patterns of an individual. Different personality theorists present their own definitions of the word based on their theoretical positions. Psychologists such as Freud, and Erik Erikson have attempted to come up with personality theories.
Death anxiety	Death anxiety is the morbid, abnormal or persistent fear of one's own death or the process of his/her dying. One definition of death anxiety is a 'feeling of dread, apprehension or solicitude (anxiety) when one thinks of the process of dying, or ceasing to 'be'. It is also referred to as thanatophobia (fear of death), and is distinguished from necrophobia, which is a specific fear of dead or dying persons and/or things (i.e. others who are dead or dying, not one's own death or dying).
Terror management theory	In social psychology, terror management theory proposes a basic psychological conflict that results from having a desire to live but realizing that death is inevitable. This conflict produces terror, and is believed to be unique to human beings. Moreover, the solution to the conflict is also generally unique to humans: culture.
Memorial service	A memorial service is a liturgical solemn service for the repose of departed in the Eastern Orthodox Church.
Lesbian	Lesbian is the term most widely used in the English language to describe romantic or sexual attraction between women. The word may be used as a noun, to refer to women who identify themselves or who are characterized by others as having the primary attribute of female homosexuality, or as an adjective, to describe characteristics of an object or activity related to female same-sex attraction. 'Lesbian' as a concept, used to differentiate women with a shared sexual orientation, is a 20th-century construct.
Anticipatory grief	Anticipatory grief refers to a grief reaction that occurs before an impending loss. Typically, the impending loss is a death of someone close due to illness but it can also be experienced by dying individuals themselves. The anticipated death can also be from non-illness-related causes such as high suicide lethality, high-risk lifestyle or gang involvement, or from non-death-related losses such as scheduled mastectomy, pending divorce, company downsizing or war.
Coping	In psychology, coping is expending conscious effort to solve personal and interpersonal problems, and seeking to master, minimize or tolerate stress or conflict.

13. Dying and Bereavement

CHAPTER HIGHLIGHTS & NOTES: KEY TERMS, PEOPLE, PLACES, CONCEPTS

Psychological coping mechanisms are commonly termed coping strategies or coping skills. Unconscious or non conscious strategies (e.g., defense mechanisms) are generally excluded.

CHAPTER QUIZ: KEY TERMS, PEOPLE, PLACES, CONCEPTS

1. _________ is the scientific study of death. It investigates the mechanisms and forensic aspects of death, such as bodily changes that accompany death and the post-mortem period, as well as wider social aspects related to death. It is primarily an interdisciplinary study offered as a course of study at numerous colleges and universities.

a. Beating heart cadaver
b. Biostratinomy
c. Thanatology
d. Body snatching

2. _________ is a multifaceted response to loss, particularly to the loss of someone or something to which a bond was formed. Although conventionally focused on the emotional response to loss, it also has physical, cognitive, behavioral, social, spiritual, and philosophical dimensions. While the terms are often used interchangeably, bereavement refers to the state of loss, and _________ is the reaction to loss.

a. Beginning of human personhood
b. Grief
c. Feticide
d. Late termination of pregnancy

3. _________ is the medical term for cessation of blood circulation and breathing, the two necessary criteria to sustain human and many other organisms' lives. It occurs when the heart stops beating in a regular rhythm, a condition called cardiac arrest. The term is also sometimes used in resuscitation research.

a. Beating heart cadaver
b. Clinical death
c. Body
d. Body snatching

4. . _________ is the particular combination of emotional, attitudinal, and behavioral response patterns of an individual. Different _________ theorists present their own definitions of the word based on their theoretical positions. Psychologists such as Freud, and Erik Erikson have attempted to come up with _________ theories.

a. 1970 British Cohort Study

b. Personality
c. Birth order
d. Casa viva

5. _________ or impotence is sexual dysfunction characterized by the inability to develop or maintain an erection of the penis during sexual performance.

A penile erection is the hydraulic effect of blood entering and being retained in sponge-like bodies within the penis. The process is often initiated as a result of sexual arousal, when signals are transmitted from the brain to nerves in the penis.

a. Beginning of human personhood
b. Definitions of abortion
c. Erectile dysfunction
d. Late termination of pregnancy

ANSWER KEY
13. Dying and Bereavement

---

1. c
2. b
3. b
4. b
5. c

---

14. Successful Aging

CHAPTER OUTLINE: KEY TERMS, PEOPLE, PLACES, CONCEPTS

______	Generation X
______	Quality of life
______	Adolescence
______	Self-efficacy
______	Body weight
______	Successful aging

CHAPTER HIGHLIGHTS & NOTES: KEY TERMS, PEOPLE, PLACES, CONCEPTS

Generation X	Generation X, commonly abbreviated to Gen X, is the generation born after the Western Post-World War II baby boom. Demographers, historians and commentators use beginning birth dates from the early 1960s to the early 1980s.
Quality of life	In general, quality of life is the perceived quality of an individual's daily life, that is, an assessment of their well-being or lack thereof. This includes all emotional, social, and physical aspects of the individual's life. In health care, health-related quality of life is an assessment of how the individual's well-being may be affected over time by a disease, disability, or disorder.
Adolescence	Adolescence is a transitional stage of physical and psychological human development that generally occurs during the period from puberty to legal adulthood (age of majority). The period of adolescence is most closely associated with the teenage years, though its physical, psychological and cultural expressions may begin earlier and end later. For example, although puberty has been historically associated with the onset of adolescent development, it now typically begins prior to the teenage years and there has been a normative shift of it occurring in preadolescence, particularly in females .
Self-efficacy	Self-efficacy is the measure of the belief in one's own ability to complete tasks and reach goals. Psychologists have studied self-efficacy from several perspectives, noting various paths in the development of self-efficacy; the dynamics of self-efficacy, and lack thereof, in many different settings; interactions between self-efficacy and self-concept; and habits of attribution that contribute to, or detract from, self-efficacy.

14. Successful Aging

CHAPTER HIGHLIGHTS & NOTES: KEY TERMS, PEOPLE, PLACES, CONCEPTS

Body weight	The term body weight is used colloquially and in the biological and medical sciences to refer to a person's mass or weight. Body weight is measured in kilograms, a measure of mass, throughout the world, although in some countries such as the United States it is measured in pounds, or as in the United Kingdom, stones and pounds. Most hospitals, even in the United States, now use kilograms for calculations, but use kilograms and pounds together for other purposes.
Successful aging	Successful aging or successful ageing (British English) refers to physical, mental and social well-being in older age. The concept of successful aging can be traced back to the 1950s, and was popularized in the 1980s. It reflects changing view on aging in Western countries, where a stigma associated with old age has led to considering older people as a burden on society.

CHAPTER QUIZ: KEY TERMS, PEOPLE, PLACES, CONCEPTS

1. In general, _________ is the perceived quality of an individual's daily life, that is, an assessment of their well-being or lack thereof. This includes all emotional, social, and physical aspects of the individual's life. In health care, health-related _________ is an assessment of how the individual's well-being may be affected over time by a disease, disability, or disorder.

   a. Quality of life
   b. Genuine progress indicator
   c. Global Liveability Survey
   d. Happy life expectancy

2. _________ is the measure of the belief in one's own ability to complete tasks and reach goals. Psychologists have studied _________ from several perspectives, noting various paths in the development of _________; the dynamics of _________, and lack thereof, in many different settings; interactions between _________ and self-concept; and habits of attribution that contribute to, or detract from, _________.

   _________ affects every area of human endeavor.

   a. Born This Way Foundation
   b. Self-efficacy
   c. Character orientation
   d. Confidence

3. . _________ is a transitional stage of physical and psychological human development that generally occurs during the period from puberty to legal adulthood (age of majority). The period of _________ is most closely associated with the teenage years, though its physical, psychological and cultural expressions may begin earlier and end later.

For example, although puberty has been historically associated with the onset of adolescent development, it now typically begins prior to the teenage years and there has been a normative shift of it occurring in pre_________, particularly in females .

a. Closed adoption
b. Deinstitutionalisation
c. Foster care
d. Adolescence

4. _________ or successful ageing (British English) refers to physical, mental and social well-being in older age. The concept of _________ can be traced back to the 1950s, and was popularized in the 1980s. It reflects changing view on aging in Western countries, where a stigma associated with old age has led to considering older people as a burden on society.

a. Biological clock
b. Successful aging
c. Calcutta Metropolitan Institute of Gerontology
d. CALERIE

5. _________, commonly abbreviated to Gen X, is the generation born after the Western Post-World War II baby boom. Demographers, historians and commentators use beginning birth dates from the early 1960s to the early 1980s.

a. 1837 generation
b. Generation X
c. Baby boomer
d. Burnt Generation

ANSWER KEY
14. Successful Aging

---

1. a
2. b
3. d
4. b
5. b

Other Facts101 e-Books and Tests

CPSIA information can be obtained at www.ICGtesting.com
Printed in the USA
LVOW10s0926020814
397232LV00002B/54/P

9 781497 001763